Ascended Masters' Messages

TREASURES
OF DIVINE WISDOM

Tatyana N. Mickushina

UDC 141.339=111=03.161.1
BBC 87.7+86.4
  M 59

M 59 Mickushina, T.N.
Treasures of Divine Wisdom

The multivolume book, *Words of Wisdom* by Tatyana N. Mickushina, has several thousand pages of text.

This book was created to meet the spiritual needs of busy people who are unable to spend much time reading.

The book includes the most concise and significant quotations from the book *Words of Wisdom*.

This book is intended for a wide audience of readers.

Copyright © T. N. Mickushina, 2017
All rights reserved.

ISBN-10: 1540815005
ISBN-13: 978-1540815002

PREFACE

This book contains priceless jewels.

The Treasures of Divine Wisdom are eternal, imperishable, and timeless. Written with the letters of fire on the scrolls of Eternity, they are now available to the artisanal miner who has dug into piles of text in order to finally find the grains of Truth.

Each person will find here exactly what he or she needs: Some will find inspiration, some will find inner peace, some will find food for thought, and some will find an answer to their questions. One should only stretch the arm and open a specific page, and read what he or she needs at that moment. What is read can later be thought over in silence and deposited into the jewel box of one's heart.

The book is comprised of concise quotations taken from the books *Words of Wisdom*, which constitute a new philosophical-moral Teaching, given to modern mankind from a Higher Source. The full collection of Divine Wisdom is available on Tatyana N. Mickushina's website: http://sirius-eng.net/dictations.

From the Editor.

Everything that is said and everything that will be said is of timeless and absolute value to you, similar to a precious pearl.

We come and present to you one pearl of wisdom after another. You yourselves string these pearls on a necklace, which you are creating throughout your entire life.

This is truly a priceless necklace of Knowledge. You should treat it with care.

Words of Wisdom

There is nothing outside of yourselves that you need. All Divine knowledge and perfection is within you. Seek this treasure in your hearts; seek this entrance to the priceless riches that reside within you.

All that you need to do is simply make a choice and step into infinity, give up the holiday festive tinsel of the past and take a step toward reality. First, take one step, and then another. Then go, without stopping, toward your real Being who you really are.

Out of all Divine qualities, the quality of Love is the greatest. The aspiration to love, the desire to love and be loved, is characteristic of all living beings.

Open your hearts to Love, the Divine Love, and you will change this world.

There is no force in this world mightier than Love.

Constantly guard your love against any manifestations of anti-love. Protect your close ones, your children. The future of the planet depends on the concept of Love that the new generation receives.

You were created in the image and likeness of God, and therefore, there is nothing impossible for you in your creativity.

Create! Build up! Aspire!
Seek and you will find.
Do not seek in the outer world that surrounds you. Look deep in your heart.
Listen to your heart.

Strive to come in contact with the subtle worlds in your heart. Begin to explore the other reality. It will come into your consciousness.

Be like children, and you will be able to reach the heights inside your consciousness that were not available to the preceding generations.

You should constantly feel inside of you the presence of two origins: the spiritual origin and the physical origin. You must constantly remember that the main part of you is the spiritual part. Your physical part is transient and necessary for you only during a particular stage of your individual evolution.

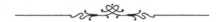

Make use of everything that helps you raise your consciousness: poetry, music, nature, playing with children, flowers. Pour the energy of your attention only onto the patterns of perfection.

Observe your feelings during the day. How often do you feel love, joy, or inexplicable high spirits? How often do you stop in the middle of the street to admire trees or clouds? How often do you go out into nature?

Listen to the sounds of nature. Look at the birds. Look at the trees. Look at the clouds. Listen to the silence.

Stay in Peace; maintain the feeling of Love and Harmony and all the rest will come to you.

God is everything. God is everything that surrounds you as far as you can see. You are God too.

You need to devote your life to God, who you are in reality. This is the task of every person.

You have to admit that if you treat yourself as God and if you treat the people around you as Gods, your life will change. The longer and more profoundly you are able to keep the image of the Deity in your consciousness, the sooner your life will change.

You simply have to guard yourself against imperfect images and surround yourself with perfect Divine images.

There are many paths and many ways leading to God. Almost each of you has your own path. However, you should never forget that there are many paths and trails leading nowhere.

God requires you to make your own efforts. The more efforts you make, the more help you will receive from above.

Maintain your balance; maintain the peace in your soul. You are warriors in this world. And just one vibration of Love and Compassion that you emanate is capable of extinguishing the fire of hell, in which many souls of this planet are burning.

People are closely interconnected in the subtle plane. A good thought, virtuous thinking originating in several minds and hearts simultaneously, is capable of spreading from heart to heart, like one candle can easily ignite a million candles with its flame.

The greatest people among you are those who do the most to serve life and all living creatures and do not demand anything for themselves in return. This is because there is nothing in this life that is worth exchanging for the gift of communion with the Divine and for the opportunity to serve God throughout your entire lives.

You know that it is always difficult for one to climb an inaccessible peak alone. But when one has climbed to the top, many can make use of his help and example and also ascend to their summits of the Divine consciousness.

Freedom is first of all a state of mind, a state of one's soul. This is the goal to which you must aspire with all your being.

Without your Faith in God none of your actions in the physical plane will be able to succeed; they will be like a house built on sand.

Only your Faith is your one guiding star that will show you the way through the storms of life that you face in the physical plane.

If you trust in God and your Faith is unshakeable, you can ask for God's guidance in your life. You will receive the guidance in the amount that corresponds to the strength of your Faith.

Your Love and your Faith are the only two things that you need to implement your Divine plan.

You will always have everything necessary to implement your Divine plan and to serve God and people, if Faith and Love become your constant companions in life, Wisdom, the Divine Wisdom, will be the attribute that you acquire when you believe and love wholeheartedly.

You worship inside your heart, and you must find God within your heart and worship only Him.
The odds are always in favor of those who are with God. It has always been this way.

Those changes on the Earth that were to take place in due time in accordance with the plan of God were not made by numbers, but by faith and devotion.

Cultivate the feeling of Love in your heart.
Your foremost task in life is to regain the feeling of Love at any price.
Love people not for something they have done or what they can do for you. Feel the Love that is unconditional.
All is God. Our separation from the Oneness with God is only in our consciousness.

In reality, everything in this Universe is God. And each of you is only a particle, a cell, an atom of this Divine body.

You should never be afraid that you will find yourselves in the wrong place. Do not be afraid to experiment. Do not be afraid to make mistakes.

You will always receive help on your path, and you can always ask for help.

Every minute and every second you live on Earth, the Divine Energy comes into your aura as a continuous flow from the Divine world. How you will use your Divine Energy depends solely on you.

Every moment of your life you make a choice, and this choice directs your Divine Energy either onto the multiplication of the illusion of this world or onto the contraction of this illusion.

You tint your Divine Energy with beautiful feelings full of joy and love, and you raise the vibration of this world.

The best sermon will be your personal example, your behavior in life, your attitude toward life's situations and tests.

Each of you must turn into a gigantic generator of Good and Light. Then there will be no place for the forces of darkness near you.

All the diversity of life and all the variety of life choices is reduced to your choice: Which world do you choose? Do you choose the illusionary world or the real world of God?

You are lonely only until you feel your unity with God within you, and through this unity you become united with everyone whose vibrations are in tune with yours.

When you love, you do not need anything else. You are ready just to experience this state and enjoy it. All your problems, all your imperfections, and the imperfections of the world around you are dissolved by this unique solvent, which is primordially inherent in this Universe.

Judge your spiritual progress not by the number of hours that you have spent in prayer and meditation. Judge your spiritual progress by the help you give to all living creatures, including people, animals, and plants. Judge your spiritual progress by the thoughts and feelings that dominate your consciousness.

These will be the fruits by which Jesus called you to judge.

You are able to grow and rise higher and higher to the summit of the Divine consciousness only by experiencing the states of constant exertion and constantly overcoming yourself.

Learn to love the exertion of all your strengths and abilities. Learn to love the aspiration and the stormy gush of obstructions that you overcome.

Bless these obstructions, bless your enemies, bless all the circumstances and difficulties of your lives because they help you to grow and overcome yourselves.

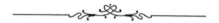

Every minute and every second of your life on Earth, you make a choice that changes not only your future but also the future of the entire planet.

The past is only given to us so that we can learn the necessary lessons from it and move forward, never stopping on the path other than for a short break to analyze the occurring events.

The potential to be God is lies within you, within each of you.

In essense, you are Gods. And your task is to gradually master your Divinity, to allow the Divinity into your external consciousness.

Do believe that you are not people who are going to play the role of God — you are Gods who have temporarily come to play the roles of people.

Your Divinity is hidden from your external consciousness, and your abilities are dormant within you until you completely fulfill your role in this world.

Your Spirit, your Divinity, and God inside of you — these are the things that you must pay attention to.

Community, Virtue, and Good will come from your hearts. Your task is simply to open your hearts and to let the Divinity in.

Learn to listen to the voices of nature; learn to contemplate nature. Learn to pass through yourself, through your consciousness, the pictures of nature that surround you.

When you are in silence on the bank of a river or at the sea shore, in a forest or in a field, you are really in the Temple of God. And you should feel complete Divine awe at God's care for you. He has built the most perfect Temples for you.

Staying in nature should be akin to visiting a temple. Thank God for every minute of silence when you are staying in His Temple and feel a reverential quiver.

It is time to return to the natural way of life provided for you by God.

Only the souls of people who are ready to communicate with the Divine world can find peace and feel bliss from contact with nature.

Learn to observe the events occurring around you as if through a screen, as though you are at the theatre and the people around you are actors.

However, the feeling of being in a play should never leave you because God has created this world as a gigantic stage where you can play your parts and go through the training at the same time.

Try not to leave the frames of the play in your life. Do not take everything around you too seriously. Always remember that the illusion around you is temporary and has been created to exist only until the moment when your consciousness is able to look behind it and see the real Divine world and the real life beyond it.

If you constantly focus your attention on the beautiful patterns of nature, music, and art, and you keep away from the imperfect, then the substitution of negative energies will take place naturally without any considerable efforts from you.

It is time for you to consciously approach everything you do during the day. You should constantly control your thoughts and your feelings.

Listen keenly to your body, and when you are overcome with depression, find a way to restore your inner harmony and peace. For some of you it will be meditating; for others it will be praying, walking in nature, listening to relaxing music, or playing with children.

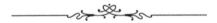

Do not worry about what will happen tomorrow and the day after tomorrow.

Do not think about what happened yesterday and the day before yesterday.

This disturbs you on your path. Think about what is happening now, and make every effort for the best service possible.

The essence of your nature is Divine. And you must return to your Divine nature.

Your search for the meaning of life in the physical plane is doomed to failure from the very start. The only true Path lies within you, inside your hearts.

All the miracles and treasures of the world are hidden in the depths of your hearts. When you manage to kindle the torch of your aspiration in your heart, everything will change within you and around you.

God allows you to experiment. Sooner or later you will be able to make certain of what among the things that you create is beautiful and harmonious and corresponds to the perfect standards and what is despicable and ugly and must be transformed.

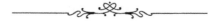

The Path to God is always only inside of you, in your hearts. You can hear the voice of God only in the stillness of your heart.

When a person becomes filled with high vibrations, when he is filled with the sense of Divine Love, he feels a causeless state of happiness and his life becomes full of meaning, peace, and harmony.

That is why it is very easy to determine the direction in which you are moving. If you experience a feeling of causeless Love, joy, and peace, then you are moving in the right direction. You are ready to embrace the entire world, and you are ready to render help to the whole world.

You are seized by causeless generosity, joy, and the desire to give out more and more of your Light and your Love, to give your Love to the world without asking for anything in return.

Any inequality, characteristic of your world, is the consequence of your imperfect consciousness. In reality, all of you are absolutely equal before your Father. The Heavenly Father loves and cares about each of you equally.

Your true enemies, with whom you must lead a merciless battle, are inside of you. And these enemies are your ignorance and your unwillingness to change your consciousness.

Even while being in an elevated state of consciousness, sweeping aside all the burdensome thoughts and feelings, you become a source of Light for your world.

Give your Love to the world. This is what you can do for the world and that does not require any extra efforts from you.

You cannot fight against the imperfection of the entire world, but you can oust all the imperfection from your world with the help of your Love.

If you wish with all your heart to change your consciousness and to raise it up to the Divine model, you must literally force yourself to give up your usual lifestyle, the standards of your behavior, and your habits.

You must become different people.

A person must discover his Divine potential and become closer to nature. Life must become as simple as possible, rich with its inner content but not with external entertainments which, if one thinks about them, resemble the entertainments of savages.

In essence, your Divine plan comes down to only one task: to keep your consciousness at the highest possible level and to aspire to reach the level of the Divine consciousness without leaving the thick of life.

Judge yourself according to the strictest laws. Work upon yourself until you overcome each of your imperfections.

The only entrance to the Divine reality is located within your heart.

Everything that surrounds you in your physical world is aimed only at helping you to evolve, to grow, and to overcome yourself, to broaden your consciousness, and to multiply your merits.

The consciousness of every human individual is the most important. Your consciousness is the thing that will outlast you, the way you are today. Your consciousness will exist in the Higher Worlds.

You receive exactly what you give to the world. If you have not performed at least one good deed during your entire life and during all your previous lives, then why do you think God will respond to your request when you are in need?

A person whose heart is an abode of God will never allow himself to do harm to another person.

You must listen to yourselves. You must sense yourselves and understand yourselves. You are not your reflection in the mirror — you are mighty spiritual beings, and the time is coming for each of you to feel it.

You are destined to win. You have no other choice but to win.

Victory is in sight!

It is the victory for those who are ready and the victory for those who are willing to accept their victory now.

A wise person always remembers that beyond the area lit by his external consciousness there is a vast field of things he is still unable to perceive.

Any task you will start to perform in cooperation is destined to be a success because it is not you who perform this task but God, who you allow to do it through you.

All your undertakings will be a success because God, whom you entrust to act through you, cannot suffer a defeat. You are destined to victory as long as you are with God!

Your consciousness is the most important thing in you. All the circumstances of your life and everything that happens to you are determined solely by the level of your consciousness. You choose whether to aspire in your consciousness to the Supreme and to progress along the Higher Path or to prefer to stagnate with a wretched existence in a cozy corner.

You are travellers who must always remain in motion and never stop. Therefore, those of you who are thinking in your consciousness that you have already attained everything and can now rest, must urgently make the necessary corrections in your consciousness. God does not have any restrictions. All the restrictions exist only in your consciousness and in your perception of the world around you.

It is always possible to find Divine manifestations in everything surrounding you in your world.

The key to your progress is inside your consciousness.

You should aspire in order to receive.

If you do not have aspirations within you, you will not be able to attract the necessary knowledge from the surrounding space.

Your consciousness and your individual experience are the main things for you. They are the things that will remain with you after your human evolution has finished. These are the things that will transit to the Higher Worlds together with you and will help you exist in those Worlds.

Only when you allow God to act through you, God uses this opportunity.

Just as the Sun bursting through the clouds is sometimes capable of sending you a ray of hope and endowing you with a feeling of love and compassion, you can give every person you meet in your life the Love from your heart.

You can wander around the valley for a long time, but we call you to the peak — to the Summit of the Divine consciousness.

To maintain attunement with the Divine and at the same time remain in the midst of life is required of you at present. Within your consciousness, you must constantly dwell on mountaintops while still feeling Earth's soil beneath your feet.

There is always the opportunity to follow the Higher Path; and there is always a chance to slide downhill.

At the moment when you make a choice in a difficult life situation, always remember that you are much more than your physical body.

Your have a Divine nature, and you are immortal. So, when making your choice always consider what will be valuable for your soul.

You should follow the Higher Path and always choose the Higher Path.

There is always an opportunity for performing a feat in your life, for selfless devotion and heroism. That is because for many people, the transformation of consciousness means literally changing their entire lives.

Each of you has moments in your life when you are given a chance to perform an action equivalent in its spiritual fullness to the deeds that the saints have performed during all times in history.

God grants everyone an opportunity to correct any mistakes. Just wish to always follow the Will of God.

God demands you in entirety. You cannot bargain with God.

Hurry up on your Path to the real world so that the gates of opportunity do not shut in your face.

Unite on the basis of Love, cooperation, and specific actions on the physical plane that you can perform right now.

Always remember that everything in this world is a mirror that reflects your consciousness, and the people around you will show the side to you that you notice in them.

Live in Joy and Love and cast away everything that hinders you from residing in God.

Always remember that thoughts materialize, and they are always capable of creating.

Learn to listen to the voice of silence coming from within you and giving you an opportunity to experience anew the bliss of fatherly love of Heavens, which Heavens are tirelessly pouring into your world.

Do not treat your planet as something permanent and given to you once and forever. Your planet, the state in which it is now, is the reflection of your thoughts, feelings, and the level of consciousness that you have now.

All great achievements started in silence during a quiet calm talk at a family hearth.

No sensible idea has ever been born in a crowd at a loud celebration.

None of the achievements in the spiritual realm that you have attained while being in the incarnation can be kept for even several months if you do not maintain your level of consciousness with everyday efforts.

There cannot be any rest in the physical octave. Only everyday work and everyday efforts.

The state of your consciousness can be maintained at the proper level only with your daily efforts. Every day you must relentlessly force yourself to work not only with your physical muscles but also with your spiritual muscles. Otherwise, they will simply deteriorate.

If you have not experienced blissful delight from contemplating nature or a child's smile, if you have lived a day without love, then you have lived that day completely in vain.

Only when you experience incomparable quiet joy and peace, you are residing in God, in the Divine state of consciousness.

Learn to constantly control your inner state and take measures to suppress any imperfect state within you.

Your task is to acquire clear vision and learn to evaluate every event and fact that you face in life.

Faith is the remedy that you need.

The first thing you should accept within yourselves is the supremacy of the Law that exists in this Universe and in your lives.

With the help of your consciousness, you are able to begin the process of recognizing and separating the Divine from the illusionary.

It is exactly in this way that you become co-creators with God. It is exactly in this way that you become able to create the Divine reality around you.

Your task is to constantly maintain a realistic viewpoint of your position in this world. Your real position is to stand with your feet firmly on Earth while at the same time remembering your cosmic origin and aspiring to God.

You came into this world to get a lesson of distinction between the Good and the Evil, the illusion and the reality.

Learn your lessons by yourselves.

Do not be afraid of any obstacles that get in your way in your world, because the obstacles indicate only that it is necessary to overcome them.

There is no other judge in your world besides yourselves. You have to learn to evaluate your deeds and thoughts on your own and get rid of all the vainity and human frailties that impede your advancement on the Path.

Your consciousness should constantly maintain the purity that is intrinsic to small children. Detach yourselves from any imperfect negative states.

Contemplate beautiful flowers and views of nature with your inner sight; listen to calm, quiet music. It will be very helpful to submerge into the contemplation of images of stars and galaxies before going to sleep. Listen and try to hear the voice of silence that comes to you from the depths of the cosmos and space.

Do not be afraid of any difficulties that you will encounter in your life. All the troubles and all the unforeseen situations are necessary and indispensable for the development of your soul. You will be unable to grow if you do not come across unforeseen situations and do not overcome the hardships of life on a daily basis.

Maintain your care about peace in your hearts. Think about the meaning of this phrase. This phrase is telling you about the peace and serenity within your hearts; this phrase is also telling you about caring for everything around you.

Your energy flows where your attention is directed. Your energy flows in the direction of your thoughts and interests.

Life does not end. Life is infinite. Life just changes into new forms.

This process is similar to perpetual motion, eternal spinning, that never ceases and never stops.

In fact, your intention is very important — what you aspire to and in what state of heart you do it, to what extent you are sincere, and to what extent you are selfless.

Listen to the call of your heart.

Seclude yourself in silence and listen to what your heart is whispering to you.

Remove all unnecessary things from your life, everything that does not give you an opportunity to stay alone and listen to the voice of your heart, to hear its tender whisper and to feel its Love.

You Love. No matter how hard you hide your Love or pretend that you do not remember your Love, it is still present within you. Your main quality is Love. Remove all unnecessary things from your life that prevent you from feeling the Divine Love in your heart.

You yourselves choose and create all the circumstances of your life.

Ignorance and lack of knowledge are the enemies that you will have to battle. Therefore, bring the Light of knowledge to the people of planet Earth. Come up, kindle your torches, and bring the Light to those who need it.

Do not feel shy about sending Love to your closest ones, for nothing is as favorable for people's souls as watering them with the energy of Love from your hearts every day.

No matter how difficult your own situation is, do not think about yourselves; think about those near you who need your care.

Sometimes, one tender look or one kind word is enough for the soul to regain hope and confidence in the future and in the meaning of life.

There is no limit to forgiveness; there is no limit to humility and compassion.

There cannot be too much of any of the Divine qualities. Your world is in such a need of Divine vibrations and Divine qualities that you can pour out your perfection, kindness, and Love all day long, and the world will be grateful to you.

You can achieve a lot, but you have to be very steadfast and brave.

The most proper thing will be to live in the present moment. The past and the future should not take up too much space in your consciousness.

You are living in the present moment, and in this moment you must always joyously face all life's difficulties and failures, and always keep confidence in your powers so that you will overcome everything and that you will come out victorious in every situation.

The Miracle of God is always ready to manifest, but only those who have the eyes of a child can see these miracles. Leave behind your grown-up games and worries. At least for a few minutes every day, let yourself return to your childhood when you expected wonders, and God performed those wonders for you in the form of sunrises and sunsets, in the form of snow, rain, and rainbows.

If you start constantly seeing God's wonders in the surrounding world, your life will begin to change significantly. You will be surprised at how much time you will have to observe the miracles of God.

No matter how grave your difficulties are, you should always remember that your existence does not end with the death of your physical body. Oh, you are far more than your physical bodies. Each of you has the potential to become a God. In the course of time, all of you will become Gods.

Everyone has their own unique manifestation of Divinity in the physical world. The main quality is your ability to feel Love for the plan of the Creator and to never stop admiring all the diversity of Divine manifestations that exist around you. Do not focus on yourselves and your problems but observe the variety and diversity of Divine manifestations and to be able to see Divine miracles and enjoy them. That is why it is said that unless you become like children, you will not be able to enter the Kingdom of Heaven.

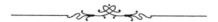

All you need is to become full of love toward life as a whole, to any manifestation of life, and to feel your Oneness with each particle of life.

Allow the Divine energy to freely flow through your being, and on its way it will wash away all small and large obstacles in the form of your ego, your fears, your limitations and dogmas.

Expose yourself to the winds of change and do not be afraid to catch a cold or fall ill.

Create the islets of Divinity and move to live there at least for some time.

In your consciousness, you must be ready for constant changes and shifts. There is nothing that will not undergo changes in the near future.

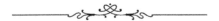

Learn to create like Gods because in the near future you will have to realize your responsibility for everything around you; and the most important thing is to realize your responsibility for the fact that you are the ones who should make changes on Earth according to the Divine models.

Do not think too much about how to support your physical existence. Think only about how to fulfill your Divine plan. Or is there so little Faith in you that you cannot believe that God will take care of you?

Consider your everyday actions. Try to analyze how long you have been thinking about God and your Divine purpose during the day. How many of you are really ready to sacrifice something for the well-being of the world?

You are the people on whom the future of planet Earth depends.

All that is genuinely from God needs your help to grow and expand.

Look around and analyze thoroughly: Out of the things that you think should be changed, what can you personally change by relying on your opportunities and your abilities?

Everything in this Universe is based on the great power of Love. Everything that exists in this Universe is there only due to the power of Love.

At the beginning of Creation, God divided his Love into an infinite number of pieces, and each of you, being a particle of God, received your own portion of Love. Now you have the opportunity to experience that Love and to refine it.

Your level of consciousness is not determined by the amount of mental information that you are able to let into your mind. Your level of consciousness is determined by the Divine qualities that you gain on your Path.

No matter how much it would seem to you that you are separated and independent, with time you will have to feel your internal unity not only with the One and indivisible Creator of this Universe but also your unity with each other.

Everything that is directed toward the convergence, the integration, and the Common Good is beneficial. Everything that is directed toward separation is subject to oblivion.

There is no place for animosity in the New World. The animosity will leave your world as your consciousness changes and grows.

All the problems of your world are in your heads, inside of you. And all the Divine perfection is also within you.

Never be saddened by your problems. Allow yourselves to be happy with the fact that by overcoming your current problems, you are preparing a bright future for yourself and your children and grandchildren.

You are given according to your Faith.

Be careful as you go through life, and think through every choice and every step that you take.

You need the gift of distinction, but sometimes you do not need any gift in order to make a distinction — you simply need to analyze your thinking, your habits, and your attachments.

Manage your monetary energy correctly. The more you give away selflessly, the more you receive.

Happiness is simply the state of your mind.

When you learn to feel joy seeing other people's achievements, you will open up an opportunity for you yourself to be successful.

True happiness lies in your ability to sacrifice yourself for the well-being of other living creatures. You sacrifice yourself, and from the point of view of the people living on Earth now, you are a failure. However, your condition resembles the state of quiet inner happiness and bliss. And you will not exchange this state for any treasures of the world.

The moment will come when your spark starts to burn, and the flames that will grow within your being will be able to light the path for many lost souls. You yourself are burning out but you light the path for others. That is why a torch or a candle is a symbol of enlightenment.

Your future is directly connected with your children. How well you manage to prepare the future generation will determine how well that generation will be able to develop Divine qualities within themselves and fulfill their Divine purpose.

God has thought through everything, and all consequences come out of their causes.

Do not rush searching for truth that comes from the human mind; strive for the Truth that is coming into your world from the Higher octaves of Light, and then you will manifest a bright future for planet Earth.

Send out your Love and Gratitude to Earth. Picture Mother-Earth as an alive being that allows you to live and grow and takes care of you.

May the world be well!

May all the living creatures inhabiting our dearly-loved planet Earth be happy. Om.

The time has come for you to treat everything that happens in your life and all your choices consciously. That is because sometimes one of your choices determines your entire future path — not only in this life but also in the course of future incarnations.

Consciously approach everything. Above all, consciously analyze your inner state and the motives that are driving you.

Never judge the people around you as to whether or not they are worthy from God's perspective. Human consciousness knows neither the level of achievements of other people nor the degree of their merits before God.

The miracles in your life have just begun. Get used to the miracles.

God grants you moments of inner silence so that you can consciously strive to repeat those states when everything within you is at peace and balance.

When the proper models of music, movies, paintings, and everything that surrounds you fill your consciousness and your surrounding environment, then you will be able to gradually overcome the negative effects of your world and transition into another, more subtle world. Your transition into the subtle world will be assured when you manage to assure the presence of the subtle world in your inner space and in your outer environment.

Proper mindset is essential. Nobody besides you will be able to overcome your imperfections and your attachments.

Use the whole array of tools that are available to you in order to constantly keep yourselves in a high state of consciousness, away from dark thoughts and feelings.

All the Divine perfection lies within you. You simply need to learn how to gain access to that perfection.

You need to learn how to part with everything that you do not need in your new life.

Do not be afraid of changes; do not be afraid to part with old habits and attachments that restrain your advancement and prevent you from breaking forth to the new level of consciousness, and you will gain truly cosmic opportunities.

You need to learn how to experience a constant feeling of inner joy, even when the external circumstances of your life unfold in the worst way possible, as it seems to you. That is because the dark period will inevitably be followed by a period of light, and the dark night will be followed by the dawn of the new day!

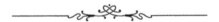

There are things in your life that lower your vibrations, and there are things in your life that raise your vibrations. That concerns everything: food, clothing, and everything around you.

Stop playing the games of yesterday and aspire to the new day with its joyful sun and fresh winds of change.

Your consciousness needs airing and drying in the sun. Remove all useless thought-forms and models from your consciousness, remove everything that is not from God, and your life will begin to change as if with a wave of a magic wand. Let yourselves become gods in manifestation. Allow yourselves joyful states of consciousness; allow yourselves to take care of your dearest ones; allow yourselves to BE and to rejoice at your life. Only when you change your approach to everything around you will all the circumstances of your life change as well.

Changing stereotypes and changing your consciousness — this is what you all will have to learn in the near future, regardless of the country and the continent where you live.

Remember and always know that you are Gods, and the next stage of your evolution is to finally become a person of reason and a person of God.

The ability to unite and perform joint work is undeniable proof that you have ascended to a new level of your consciousness.

All of your accomplishments must be manifested in the physical plane. Your main accomplishment is the ability to collaborate and fulfill concrete work on the physical plane.

There is a lot of work in your world, and all that work is done by those who have attained certain spiritual accomplishments instead of just thinking that they have accomplished something.

Your aspirations will yield results much faster if you apply all the acquired knowledge in your daily life as soon as you receive it. Whatever does not get reinforced in practice becomes useless, dead knowledge.

If you have chosen the Path and you tirelessly follow it every day, then very soon all that is unnecessary and all that impedes you will be cast away by you as something that is useless and burdening to you on the way.

Only your qualities that are Divine and eternal will remain.

The whole distinction, the entire mechanism of distinction, is hidden inside of you, within your hearts. All of you are created in the image and likeness of God. You can hear in your hearts only the things that you are ready and waiting for.

All the Divine is very simple. This simplicity frightens off and causes doubt in those who still search for complicated paths and voluntarily drive themselves into the maze of the teachings that lead nowhere but toward the death of the soul.

Always remember that the Knowledge is given to you for reflection and meditation in the stillness of your heart.

You should tirelessly purify your subtle bodies with prayer and fasting, with walks in nature, and by association with children and animals. Contemplate on beauty, and under the influence of beauty you will change your inner state. Nothing has the same effect on a person as beauty and nature. Preserve and cultivate proper models in your lives. Try to have everything that surrounds you fill you with harmony and beauty.

All the wonders that happen have been carefully planned. The miracle of the transformation of the physical plane will inevitably happen, but in order for it to happen, you need to prepare that miracle in your hearts.

You know all the decisions within your hearts.

Your God the Father is a very caring and loving parent. In this respect, you are very lucky to have your Father in Heaven because He loves you greatly, and He cannot allow you to go on doing harm to your soul. Trust your Father and humbly submit to His Will.

The time has come when you, each of you, must follow the commandments given by the prophets, the commandments of the Law that were written on the stone tablets in the days of Moses.

The time has come not to just talk about God but to act according to the Divine Law in your lives.

Be on your best behavior when you are alone with yourself, just as you would behave in front of other people, and behave toward other people just as you would behave if you had God the Father in front of you.

Always remember that your own behavior in life, the way you react to certain life situations and problems, serves as the best example. All of your actions will constitute your preaching. By the fruits of your actions, people will recognize in you a person who is worth listening to and one who should be consulted.

The time has come to think about returning to the spiritual world. It is time to think about your Father's Home, the House of the Father, from which all Creation began and where everything must return.

How often in your life do you think about the Eternal? How often do you strive to understand who you really are — not the person who you are in this life according to your profession or your relationships with other people? How often do you think about your spiritual growth, about your Heavenly Parents, about where you are going and where your Source is?

The time has come to do Good. The time has come for you to consciously choose the Good and follow it in your lives.

You are the cells of a single organism of this Universe. That is why the entire success of your work and the timeframe of its implementation depend on the extent to which you properly function in accordance with the Divine plan.

Stop considering yourselves as something separate from God. Feel your Oneness with all of life at least for a short while. Imagine that people on the other side of the globe can perish because of one of your negative thoughts or because of a wrong choice you make.

Divine solutions come only when you reject the earthly human logic and dedicate your entire self, your whole being, to serving the Supreme Law.

Selflessness, devotion, love, compassion, divine mercy, charity, and purity are qualities in the Divine World that you can keep with you. However, in order to possess these qualities, you have to develop them in your physical manifested world.

It is time to remember your true Home and your Divine purpose.

God sees everything and it is impossible for you to hide from Him even the slightest movement of your soul.

It would be nice for you to make it a rule to constantly feel the presence of an invisible witness near you who is watching your actions and even the workings of your soul.

Simply perform good actions and do not think about the reward.

Do not try to change the people who are close to you, but try to change yourself, and those people will have to adjust to the new stereotype of behavior adopted by you.

You simply need to change your own stereotypes of behavior and, with your own example, show others how to do it.

The new time will be different due to the implementation of the Divine principles in the behavior of each family member. You will be surprised to find out that your relationships with other people will hardly be different from those that are practiced in your family.

Please understand that it is enough for just a small percentage of planet Earth's population to get new ideas and to expand their consciousness to the necessary level, and the whole planet will be taken over by new thinking and new vibrations.

Your inner work on self-perfection always means only the realization of yourself as the Divine manifestation and giving up everything within you that is not of the Divine.

When you are calm, peaceful, and filled with Divine tranquility in your heart, nobody in the world will be able to convince you that you have found the wrong God. It is impossible to confuse it with anything else.

Each of you must come to God. Each of you will inevitably come to your God who is residing on the throne of your heart.

When you are able to bring the Divine models into your life, you will be able to feel fulfillment and harmony.

Now is a very difficult time when literally every person makes considerable changes to the situation on planet Earth by his or her choices.

The only thing required of you is just to make the decision and act in accordance with the Divine principles in your lives.

The New Day is coming, and that Day is characterized by the lack of limitations, by the Divine Freedom, and by the Divine Love.

Nothing should interest you other than your relationship with God. When you are seeking God in order to find the meaning of life and begin to teach this meaning to others, you do not come to God; instead you are distancing yourself from Him.

Only when you find complete satisfaction in communication with God within you, and you do not need to share your quiet joy with anybody because you are completely satisfied and happy, only then will you find true God.

There is always room for heroism in your life. Your heroism will not be appreciated by the external consciousness of people, but your heroism will be appreciated in Heaven.

You are required to submit to the Higher Law and to have the desire to follow the Path of evolutionary development. For this you need to reconsider your life and your attitude toward life.

It is necessary to raise your level of consciousness to the point when you understand that by doing something for your neighbor you actually take care of yourself.

You must comprehend the simple truth that there is nothing in your world that can be the meaning of your life, because your world has been created for a while, for that period of time during which you must learn your lessons and mature.

Only based on the feeling of Divine Love, are you able to comprehend the Truth. This is the Law that works unalterably when the energy is being exchanged between the octaves.

Your perfection in God is not possible if you cannot develop this quality of Divine Love within yourselves.

You should feel the unconditional Love that is not related to a particular person but is more general. You should love each being in your world and every being in the Divine world.

You should start and do everything in your lives only with the feeling of Love.

First of all, you must bring the Divine consciousness and the Divine patterns to that place on the globe where you live, to your family, and to your workplace. You and only you are able to bring the new consciousness into the world.

You must realize the whole greatness of the work that you are to do. You must consciously stand up for the Divine patterns in everything: in morality, in ethics, in the areas of education, religion, and healthcare. Every sphere of human activity needs changes. It will be a revolution in consciousness.

You should defend for the Divine patterns of behavior without getting involved in the conflict. You have to defend the Divine Law. You will have to demonstrate this Law in your lives.

You are required to repeat the feat of Christ when He chose to go through His crucifixion instead of standing up to the Law with a weapon in His arms.

Every one of you must be ready to sacrifice yourselves without violating any of the Divine Commandments recorded by Moses on the tablets.

Remember, always remember, that it is not the work itself that is important, but the impulse, the momentum that you put into your action in the physical plane.

If you put the whole momentum of Love that you have, if you perform a very small task with great Love, then your contribution is capable of changing a lot on planet Earth.

You should learn practical work that is aimed at the transformation of your physical world.

The requirement of a prayer before completing a specific task is still valid. This is because when you are in a prayerful state of consciousness, you are capable of harmonizing yourselves and completing the given task in the best way possible.

God does not want you to suffer. God wants you to learn the lessons of your past mistakes and not to repeat them.

As long as you keep your consciousness concentrated on the Divine world and feel invincible, you have nothing to fear.

The whole battle and the whole victory lie within you. The Armageddon is happening in your hearts. The separation of the wheat from the chaff is happening in your hearts.

All your actions in the physical plane require checking against the inner compass stored within your hearts.

Everything will change around you as soon as you change the vector of your aspirations, as soon as you make a choice to strive for Divinity and throw aside the cast-offs of your former attachments.

Of course, you need to have a very high self-conceit to think that you are doing everything in your lives by yourselves and manage everything yourselves. You manage your lives exactly to the extent that the Divine Law allows.

If you do not encounter any changes in your lives either yesterday, today, or tomorrow, it means only one thing: Your consciousness is not changing.

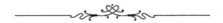

You need to know how to set priorities in your life. There are primary and there are secondary tasks. There are eternal tasks, there are the tasks of the current incarnation, and there is the daily fuss.

You need to love yourselves not as a physical body but as the manifestation of God on Earth.

Do not be afraid to be left alone with yourself. Learn how to listen to the silence and enjoy the solitude.

You should not fear anything. You should always remember in your consciousness that you are immortal and that God is taking care of you.

It is necessary for you to understand that there is a whole universe beyond the borders of your dense world.

You will accomplish everything and your Victory will come to you.

You should simply maintain the aspiration to the Higher worlds in your hearts. You should constantly try to overcome Earth's gravity of the surrounding illusion.

There is nothing more significant that can help you on your Path of ascension to the Summit of the Divine consciousness than helping the ones close to you. You can even not follow the Path yourselves but instead help the people around you to follow it, and together with them you will overcome all the obstacles and difficulties on your Path.

You know that theory without practice is dead. When you only study some science or literature without putting it into practice, you do not advance anywhere. It is similar to running in place.

First, you realize in which direction you should go, and then you begin to understand what in your lives prevents you from following the set direction. Then you begin to overcome one obstacle after another in your lives.

First you remove the wrong quality from your consciousness, then your life changes in proportion to the efforts that you make in the right direction.

Take action, make mistakes, redo, but continue your efforts.

You know that your victory over death is inevitable if only you are able to elevate your consciousness to the level of your immortal part.

There are always people who carry the fire in their hearts and are ready to serve humanity.

You must always be aware of your connection with many, many souls of Light on the planet. Together you form the network of Light that is dispersed around the planet.

All your ordinary work should be set on the new foundation and done in accordance with the Divine principles.

You need to shift the priorities in your daily life and do everything at a new angle — the angle of service to the Common Good, to the work of the Masters, and to the evolution of planet Earth.

God requires you whole. All your life must be devoted to the Divine Service.

You have to work tirelessly if you wish your development to go on rising right to the top of Divine consciousness.

As soon as you allow yourself to relax a little, you roll down to the foot of the mountain.

All that was in the past is left in the past. You must think about the present and about what you are to do now and how you can carry out your Service.

Nothing in this Universe happens randomly. Everything is subject to the strict Law.

There are no borders on the subtle plane. If you look at Earth from space, you also will not see any borders on it except the borders of the continents. Boundaries are located only within your consciousness, and all the limitations of your consciousness must be eradicated.

All that is required of you is not to submit yourselves to the influence of the lower, non-divine models and manifestations but to saturate your lives with Divine models and manifestations.

Do not be greedy with the energy of your prayers and do not be greedy with your Love, which you send to everything around you. Every particle of the energy you send is carefully saved, and it is used for the good of the evolutions of planet Earth.

All the efforts that you apply are never lost. Imagine the angels who collect every particle of the energy of Love and Gratitude that you send to Heaven.

You should gradually transition to greater Oneness and Unity.

In order to continue your existence, you must transition to the new level of consciousness, to the level that will allow you to experience your Oneness with every particle of Life.

When you reach the highest point of understanding Unity with every particle of Life, you realize that you are not something detached from the whole Creation. You are this whole Creation, and if a part of you dies, then you still continue to Live.

May the Earth live.

May the world be well.

May all living beings be happy.

It is important that God dwells in the hearts of every human living in the world. It is important that every human lives in accordance with the Law.

Try to follow the inner need of reflection in your heart.

The liberation from bad habits, illnesses, or stable negative states does not make any sense if you do not use the released time, energy, and power to perform the deeds of God in your physical octave.

You should concentrate your attention on the implementation of concrete deeds in the physical plane and start fulfilling them. Not global actions, but small steps in the right direction are needed.

You will not be able to go uphill with a backpack filled with junk. Leave all unnecessary things and habits behind, and let God take care of you.

Only complete harmony and balance between the spiritual and the physical with a slight predominance of spiritual interests can manifest the necessary result in the physical world.

You will not be able to take the right actions in the physical plane and make the right decisions if you do not maintain your consciousness in attunement with God.

You only need to allow God within you to manifest Himself.

Only when you become like little children and believe in the miracles that come to you from our world will these miracles manifest themselves on your physical plane and in your lives.

There are always pioneers who begin a difficult and important task. The majority will stand aside and watch anxiously to see what happens in the end.

Everything will end very well for your planet! The Earth will live and thrive!

You become what you aspire to. Do not forget this simple Truth. Your world is a reflected world, and it obediently mirrors your consciousness.

Only faith in God and love for the entire Creation are able to save mankind in the near future.

You are able to build true relationships in your world only based on the feeling of unconditional, endless Love.

There is a non-manifested particle of God in every one of you, and the task of each of you is to manifest God, to give God the opportunity to act through you.

Maintain the proper state of consciousness during the entire day, day after day, year after year, and you will reap an unprecedented harvest from your spiritual attainments.

The only thing for the sake of which you should be living is the development of your Divine qualities.

There is always a place for heroic acts in your lives, and there is always a place for manifesting knight-like heroism and devotion to the cause that you are serving.

The border between the worlds is inside you. And you alone move this border in your consciousness.

You are all connected with each other on the subtle plane, and each victory of yours becomes a joint victory and spreads to the most remote places on the globe.

Every one of you should aim at being a good influence on every person you meet during the day.

You need to ascend to the stage from where you can see the Oneness of not only all the religions existing in the world but also of all the people living on the planet.

God and the adherence to His Law should occupy the central place in your life.

You should not have any idols in your life that you would worship more than God.

You should not treat others in the way you do not wish them to treat you.

You should not perform any deeds that contradict the Divine Law that exists in this Universe.

The first and the main commandment is to Love your neighbors, and not only for those who are dear to you but also the whole Creation, everything created by God: a stone, a plant, any beast and animal. You should not do harm to nature. You should not do harm to Earth.

You should Love the whole Creation.

Most of all, you should treasure the moral Law in your hearts: Do not allow adultery, do not covet your neighbor's goods[1], do not lie, do not envy, be sincere and truthful.

Now it is a new time, and your responsibilities before God and before his whole Creation are increasing manifold.

You should grow the sprouts of this new consciousness within yourself. You should grow a feeling of Oneness with all of life within yourself.

Your task is to find a way to make the new things fit in with the existing ones, to gradually substitute the old patterns with the new ones.

---

[1] "Do not covet your neighbor's goods" means do not wish for anything that belongs to another person including everything that is their legal property, their personal belongings, as well as any merits, such as good luck, etc.

Remember that energy is flowing in the direction of your attention. Therefore, always try to direct this energy at creating the right patterns in your world.

Try to trust your heart, and you will be surprised to learn that your heart always gives you hints. These prompts are inevitably correct in directing you in your life.Remember that every word and thought of yours shakes the space of planet Earth.

Everything is very simple. You need to gradually give up the wrong patterns and manifestations and surround yourselves with proper Divine patterns and manifestations. You need to do that by yourselves.

As soon as you make the right aspiration and ask God for help, God will send you both the opportunity and the means for the realization of your aspiration.

You yourselves create your future. You do it every day, every minute, and every second.

Follow the Divine Law and the circumstances of your life will change!

Do not be afraid to give up everything and follow God. God will take care of you. Do you really think that you will be left without care and support if you aspire to God with sincerity and devotion?

If you start thinking about changing your entire lifestyle more often, you will soon see real changes in the circumstances of your life.

At the time when you think about your heart, you start attuning yourself to the Divine Reality because you know that the beats of your heart measure off of the Eternity.

In fact, society makes progress only when Divine Wisdom prevails in the mass consciousness, and the Divine Law gradually becomes the main Law to which your whole life and the life of the country in which you live obey.

The state of Divine Bliss can only be acquired by constant efforts aimed at the Service to Life.

When you consciously consider everything that you do, when you keep track of every choice and action of yours and evaluate it against the Divine Law, then you come closer to God.

Only a few people always started great deeds, and then millions joined them.

Where there is God, there is only giving — you are being given, again and again, the Divine nectar and are not asked for anything in return.

Live simply. Follow the commandments given by Moses and the prophets and, above all, try to maintain in your heart the feelings of Love and compassion toward your neighbor and all living beings.

When Love lives in your heart, you do not need any external preacher, you do not need to spend your time on searching for God outside of yourselves because you have Love, and therefore, you reside in God because God is Love.

There is nothing in your world that will not cause consequences. Each action causes a consequence.

All things must pass, and each obstacle is given to you only to strengthen the muscles of your soul.

Each minute must be filled with real meaning, and the energy must be directed toward creating models in the physical plane that can be multiplied and spread around the world.

It is necessary to unite all forces, it is necessary to perform specific tasks, and it is necessary to have your help and participation!

Consolidated and concise actions are required. Everything that can be saved and transferred to the New World must be saved now.

It is not a one-time act of giving your life as a sacrifice for the Common Good that is required of you. You must turn your entire life into an act of selfless service and self-sacrifice.

Do not be afraid of the difficulties that are bringing along the changes. All the old and useless things will have to be taken to the dump of history. All that is impeding you will have to be taken away from the Path and burned in the cosmic oven.

Welcome to the radiant tomorrow! Do not forget, however, that this radiant tomorrow will be built with your help, with your hands and feet, with the aspiration of your hearts!

The doors of the cosmic opportunity are wide open. Yet, try to pass through these doors with your heads high, your shoulders straightened, and accompany your procession with joyful smiles.

If you do not take at least one little step forward, you will fall behind more and more, and you risk missing the Divine opportunity that is opening up.

Your salvation is that you will be able to constantly experience the elevated states of consciousness. When your vibrations are high, you maintain harmony with the Higher worlds, and it is easier for you to retain the orienting points in your lives.

Your world needs Light, Love, high vibrations of the Higher octaves, and each of you, my beloved, can serve as a source of joy, happiness, Light, and Good for your world. The only thing you should do is to make the decision and help everyone who needs your help, not for the sake of gratitude but as an urge of your heart, of your soul.

Your world needs conductors of the Divine energy.

By overcoming yourself, you are changing the external situation, and you are changing your world.

We are giving you the knowledge and information that are vital for you. We provide you with information, and each time you have a chance to receive a new pearl.

After some time passes, you will discover with amusement that the pearls we have given you are enough to make a necklace. You will wear this necklace until the end of your embodiment. It will impart its warmth to you and give you strength during the moments when your mind is filled with doubts about the chosen Path, and the troubles of life wrap around you in a tight ring of returning karma.

Words of Wisdom

Note that the essence is not in the tempo at which you move but in your constancy and in following the same landmarks.

If your thoughts are pure, then the actions that you perform in the physical plane will also comply with the Divine Law.

You are able to do much more than you do now. We expect you to become living role models in life. Start the process of transformation from yourself.

Everything that surrounds you has much more influence on you than you can imagine. Therefore, surround yourself with proper models, try to reside in a harmonious environment, and then many of your psychological problems will either leave you or will be weakened to the extent that they will not dispirit you.

In order to carry the Light to your world, you need to gain consonance with the Light.

Compassion and mercy are manifested not only in your care about your neighbors. These qualities of your heart are cosmic in nature and should spread to all living beings. Your care for all living beings should be exacly the same as your care for your own mother.

When the world is ruled by just these two qualities — compassion and mercy — negative manifestations of human consciousness such as wars, acts of terrorism, and hatred will leave this world. Many other negative qualities that are present in mankind now will also perish.

The main things that will be left is your care of all living beings and your Love toward any Divine manifestation.

When true mercy and compassion become constant companions of the majority of mankind, sufferings will gradually leave your world.

Stop playing gods. Just be gods.

You should make humility before the Supreme Law your priority.

Be wiser, be braver. Do not be afraid to defend your views and beliefs, even if they contradict the views of the people who live near you.

You should be guided by the highest wisdom in your lives and follow the Supreme Path!

Go along the Supreme Path!

There is a mechanism that exists in your hearts, and this mechanism always knows in which direction you are moving. When you are moving toward the Light, you have no doubts.

The New Time has come, the Time for those who are daring, who are open, energetic, and hard-working.

Hurry so that you do not miss the Divine opportunity! Hurry to take your step into the New World!

You need to find a point of quietness and tranquility, of calmness and peace within you, in which God abides. From this point, you should try to understand that there is nothing in your physical world that can harm you and harm your soul unless you wish to succumb to panic mode and rush to save yourself.

Are you doing everything you can?

Are you able to wake up and direct at least one soul in your surroundings?

Try to realize that your invulnerability is directly connected with your Faith and devotion, with how much you can obey the Divine Law of this Universe.

Everything can be changed, but one needs to know where to aspire and how to achieve it.

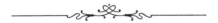

Heavens always provide help. Even when you think that everything is hopeless, there is always an opportunity to solve the problem in the Divine way. You just need to believe and make your own efforts to solve the problem.

In order to make a Divine choice, you do not need to shout about it. You make your choice in your hearts, and you make it literally every minute of your stay on Earth.

The time has come for you to act because the harvest that Death reaps and the harvest that Life reaps depend on each of you.

Do not fall for exquisite trinkets and do not enter the pavilions where your most priceless treasure — your soul — is seized from you during a loud celebration.

The only place where you can feel comfortable and where you can come in contact with Eternity is inside your heart.

There, inside of you, the worlds come together. There, inside of you, you are able to gain peace, even when the storms of your time are knocking you down.

The Divine Truth is simple. The Divine Love is open to all. Everything lies at the surface, and you do not need to pay money for the Divine Wisdom. God gives everything to everyone for free.

You just need to find the narrow path leading you to the Divine Summit among thousands of roads and highways leading to dead ends.

The Truth, God, and Love do not abide outside of you — they abide inside of you.

Accept within your hearts and try to manifest the Great Divine Law in your lives.

Only the eternal will remain. The best manifestations of your Spirit, selflessness, sacrifice, devotion, the highest manifestation of Love, and many other things will exist with you in the New World. When the old world moves to non-existence, the New World will take its place.

Trust in the Great Law of this Universe. Nothing will happen to those who believe, to those who love, to those who have hope.

God is with you! Do not be afraid of the changes!

Never stop aspiring. Never allow the illusion to capture your consciousness completely.

The time has come when you have to separate the wheat from the chaff in everything that surrounds you and reject everything that is not divine.

Realize that the present time is such that not a single minute can be lost. You have no time to postpone the work on changing yourselves, on changing your consciousness.

Do not expect a miracle to come from the outside. If you are not ready inside of you, no miracle can help you.

Lead by example! Be brave, be enduring, and be inventive. Invent the ways that will carry millions of people to a new level of consciousness. Make yourself sound as the highest note. Be the example!

You are invincible and invulnerable as long as you keep your consciousness at the Divine level.

All that you are required to do now is to clothe yourselves in the real Divine consciousness and to not lose the level of your consciousness throughout the day and day by day.

The time in which you live now is unforgettable! No matter how hard it is for you, you need to realize that it is necessary to endure and it is necessary to withstand. You cannot fall into despondency! Learn to love the stress, learn to love the battle!

It is said that only the bravest and the most devoted ones will be able to continue the evolution.

God is ever present in your world, but you should observe it. God is present within each of you. You need to observe it.

Your level of consciousness is determined by the Divine qualities that you acquire on your Path. It is impossible to fake Service, self-sacrifice, selflessness, or Love.

You must master these qualities, and they must become inherent in you.

The whole mechanism and the key to changing your consciousness are hidden inside of you. You only have to realize the new principles that inevitably have to replace the old ones that society is currently based on. You have to realize that such qualities as Love, Mercy, and Compassion are not something abstract. These are the qualities that must come into the life of every person who wishes to continue the evolution on planet Earth. It is enough for you just to feel constant thirst and need for change. You must aspire with all your being to the future world, the world free of imperfections and vices that are inherent in mankind at the current stage.

You are trying to find happiness outside of yourself. Yet, happiness is the state of your consciousness. When you are truly happy, you need nothing; you are satisfied and ready to share your joy with the whole world.

Stop and think. Your world obediently conforms to your consciousness. You receive from the external world exactly what you aspire to.

In reality, all the road signs are within you. If you listen to your inner voice carefully, you will soon know where the Divine Path lies.

You will not come across the direction signs of the Divine Path anywhere. However, the compass and the map of the Divine Path are always present in your hearts from birth until the transition.

Do not strive to walk a broad road that leads nowhere. Walk along the narrow, hardly distinguishable path that will lead you to the eternal Life.

Do not strive to solve everything in one stroke. Small, yet continuous efforts that you apply in the right direction lead to the best results.

If you are sincerely glad about the achievements of somebody else, then with this, you acquire the whole momentum of the merits of this person.

The border of the Divine world lies inside your hearts.

One cannot say that God is unjust. Everyone makes their choices by themselves. At the subconscious level, everyone is aware of the choices they make.

You judge yourself and make a choice on your own. God does not impede you.

When the hearts are talking, the mind is silent.

Your task is to raise your consciousness as high as possible to the sphere where there are no contradictions between people.

This secret should be told to as many people as possible — immediately! The secret is that as soon as you let God be present within you, you change everything around you.

You, each of you, let God be present within you!

All areas of human life are determined only by the extent to which people let God be present within them.

God gives you energy so that you can fill those who are in need with it, those who need your help and support for further wending through life.

Your smile doesn't cost anything, your love doesn't cost anything, and your friendliness doesn't cost anything. God gives you all that. And you must bring all this to the world.

True values exist! There is something for the sake of which you have come into embodiment and to which your everyday efforts must be directed.

Be brave to give up your affection to the "blessings" of your civilization, and you will gain genuine blessings and everlasting values.

Nature abhors a vacuum, and each of your negative qualities will be replaced by a Divine one, and your human affections will be replaced by a state of Divine peace, harmony, tranquillity, happiness, and joy. This is exactly what you lack in your lives.

Truth and knowledge are not bought for money. They enter your being when your consciousness is ready to comprehend them.

This happens inevitably.

You and God. How often can you be face to face with God and speak with Him?

It is not meant for you to understand the plan of God with your human consciousness. You simply need to obey God's Law and follow Him dauntlessly.

You can gain your immortality and the transition to the New World only when keeping the inner devotion to God and the Supreme Law.

You should understand that God can transform the physical plane of planet Earth only with your help, since each of you is a necessary element in the Divine chain.

Your inner choices determine the future of mankind, which may change any moment if only a certain number of the light-bearers manifest their Oneness and aspiration.

Your inner world, your harmony with the Divine world, will eventually determine your future and the future of your planet.

The Law of space and the physical world is such that you get exactly what you strive for. You can do anything in your world. You are gods in your world.

It is time to wake up to the Higher Reality of Being. Awaken! Prepare yourselves for the perception of new energies and new vibrations!

The inner worship of God is as necessary for you as the air to breathe. If you do not manage to cultivate this feeling of the Divine within yourself, then you will not be able to move any further. Your advancement along the path of evolution is inseparably connected with the extent to which you admit Divinity into your consciousness.

The feeling of Love, the most elevated feeling of Love that you can experience, resembles the Divine feeling.

Only the models of Light, only beauty must occupy the primary place in all the mass media, and in particular on TV and on the Internet.

Everything can still be corrected! Devotees of Spirit are needed! Creators and Makers are needed!

You must have careful attitudes not only to children. Every person living in the physical world has the right to be loved.

Only when you constantly experience Love, joy, and elevated states of consciousness are you in the Divine state of consciousness.

The level of your consciousness is not determined by the number of prayers you uttered or by the number of times you visited temples and holy places. The level of your consciousness is determined by the perfect states of joy, inner tranquility, and peace.

There have never been great achievements of spirit among crowds of people. All great deeds of spirit have been done in silence, in candlelight, and in prayer. You ascend within yourselves. You mount the steps leading upwards.

You need not seek outside yourselves what is necessary for your spiritual growth. Seek within yourselves; there is the door leading to eternity.

You should always remember that God does not give you unrealistic tasks and that any task or problem that you are faced with, even if it blocks your entire vision, is only an illusion. The problem continues to appear only until you, in your consciousness, find the key to its solution.

If you constantly concentrate on problems, you will encounter problems, while if you concentrate on success, success will always accompany you!

Learn how to look upon each situation from the positive side. It is important to find a correct point of view to look upon your situation.

You should pay more attention to working on yourselves. The whole perfection is already inherent in you. This is your Divine essence, the gold that lies in the depths of your being.

Your creative power, your creative abilities, and your health depend directly on your ability to control your sexual energy.

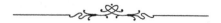

Look around and see how many things can be done. One life is not enough to get everything done. Catch the current of the Divine opportunity. Begin with the project that lies right in front of you.

Be persistent in attaining your set goals, and always remember that by performing collaborative work in the physical plane, you approach the blessed days when it will be possible to realize the Golden Age on Earth.

The surrounding area of the place where the result of collaborative work of many people is manifested in the physical plane is purified in the same way as if you were praying from dawn until dusk.

Any task, even the smallest and most insignificant that you do in your lives can be done with great Love.

God has already taken care of everything. You have the best conditions to start your service and to work on the qualities that prevent you from manifesting Love and care to your neighbors in the most difficult life situations. Until you learn to find great service in the little nothings of life, you will not be able to progress along the Path.

Every time before you start doing something, think about what really drives you. Is it the desire to prove something to others, to show your greatness, or to show everyone your diligence? Are you driven by Love for your neighbor, which is inherent in you and affects everything you do? Very simple things that you perform selflessly with great unconditional Love remain with you forever as the treasures of your causal body. Your earthly life will pass, but your attitude toward the tasks and people will remain and will accompany you in your next incarnation.

You need to think more about what prevents you from manifesting Divine qualities in your life, and gradually, step by step, get rid of everything that impedes you.

May all your progress along your life be accompanied only by Love and the fragrance of roses!

The qualities of spirit are not manifested among the crowds of people but in your everyday life. You either possess the perfect qualities or you try to master them, or you live like an animal, thinking only about the satisfaction of your needs.

The flames of your spirit and the flame of your heart should concern you first and foremost. You should not be concerned about the things that belong to your world. Only the qualities of the spirit are important.

A person is climbing a vertical cliff without safety equipment. Yet, all those who wish to follow him get the rope of help and support, and so the Path feels much easier to them.

Your consciousness is just a ticket into the eternal world. A person who can blossom as a beautiful lotus of the Divine consciousness in the swamp of life deserves to enter into the eternal Life.

Do not collect the treasures that belong to your world; collect only the treasures of Divine Wisdom that have value in all the worlds.

First of all, your consciousness must be liberated. You need to learn to feel a sense of Divine freedom in your consciousness as non-attachment to the material world.

The consonance with the Divine world, even for a short period during the day, allows your soul to taste the food that is so necessary for it. Your soul is nourished by the Divine bliss; and you must pay attention to your soul.

The manifestation of Faith and virtue is necessary everywhere, in every town and in every village. Only true Faith can open the Divine opportunity — but not the pretense of faith, which is worthless.

The issue is entirely in your consciousness and in what you are able to accept in your consciousness.

You need to develop sensitivity to the subtle manifestations in life. Do not think about what is imperfect. Start creating.

Learn to see the perspective in your advancement, and learn to feel the direction in your aspirations.

All human activities should be accompanied by Divine inspiration. Regardless of what you do, you should do it with joy and inspiration.

You must surround yourselves with beautiful models in your life: with soft enchanting music and refined forms.

You need to instill the taste for beauty in the new generation of people from childhood. The sense of beauty, the knowledge of proportions, and the sense of tact in communication not only with people but also with the representatives of the subtle world should be taken in by the new generation of people with their mother's milk.

Only the call for the Light forces that you make every day, several times a day before starting any activity (work, home chores, education), is capable of changing your life completely in a little while and fill it with Light and inner sense.

Do everything that is in your power to fill the space around you with perfect models.

Joy is a state of consciousness that is not attached to the physical world. It is the consciousness where the Higher worlds are reflected

Joy and Love. It is enough for you to cultivate only these two qualities within yourselves, and you will see how everything will start changing in your life.

Reshape your consciousness. First, accept the Divine principles and the Divine models in your own mind, and then spread these models into your world.

Each of you has Life as your teacher. Depending on how you treat all the problems and situations that evolve in your life, you may either move forward on the path of evolution or fall far behind.

You need to understand that there is nothing more important in your lives than your relationship with God — your personal relationship with God.

God does not belong to any religion, faith, or nationality. God is great! He is everything that surrounds you, everything that you see and that you do not see.

The only way out that God is leaving for you is the strong Faith, unconditional Love, and Divine Wisdom that is coming from your hearts.

Love is the key, and by manifesting only this quality you can attain Divine Truth and strengthen your Faith. While doing so, you are experiencing only Love and rejoice in following your Path.

You need to remember that God is the most important in your life, and devote all your life only to the fulfillment of God's plans.

There is always room for heroic acts in your lives. You perform a heroic act every day when you perform God's work on Earth, despite any external circumstances, despite feeling unwell, despite any illnesses.

God has taken care of everything already. All you need to do is open your eyes and see the work that you need to start doing.

Your hearts contain the mechanism that allows the Divine opportunity to manifest itself in the physical world.

Therefore, it is the flames of the spirit and the flames of the heart that need to be ignited by you.

Being in God is natural for your souls. This is what you endlessly long for and seek for in your world.

The understanding of eternal Life and gradual separation from everything that is not eternal is what should concern you first and foremost. When you are directing yourselves toward the Light, when you know that you are ever-living and have only made a temporary stop on this planet, then you are moving along the Path to God.

All that is eternal within you is your consciousness and the best life experiences that you are able to gain.

The manifestation of your best Divine qualities, such as self-sacrifice, selflessness, unconditional Love and compassion — all of these remain with you as the achievements of your spirit.

You do not need to seek proof of God's existence, and you do not need to waste energy on proving the existence of eternal Life to yourselves. There is a Path that lies in your hearts. God took care so that each of you could have direct access to the Divine world through your personal mystical experience, through your personal contact with the Eternal.

There is God's plan, and it must be fulfilled.

Donations are very similar to prayers. The more selflessly you donate the energy, the more gifts you will receive in the future.

Remember, it is not you who earns the money in exchange for labor — it is God who grants you the money. Therefore, it is pointless to make money.

When God comes to live in your heart, you do not need anything anymore. You experience full satisfaction, and God takes care of you.

There are things in your lives that are eternal — for example, beauty, Love, harmony, and peace. Divine Truth is also part of the chain of these imperishable values.

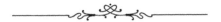

You finally have to take full responsibility for everything that takes place on the planet. You have to stop acting like children and grow up.

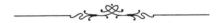

To keep up with the times, you will have to get rid of the old load that lies on your shoulders as a burden that does not let you take a single step forward. Be brave and throw aside all your attachments, your habits, all that lowers your vibrations. You will understand where to go and what to do as you go.

As long as God lives in your heart, as long as you are cheerful and friendly, as long as you believe and love, you will not be afraid of anything!

Leave the past behind you. The New Day and the new Divine opportunity await you!

The main Law of this Universe is Service to your neighbors and Compassion and Mercy on the basis of unconditional Love and selflessness.

This is a given, the conditions that were predetermined when this Universe started the cycle of its existence.

The only thing that can save humanity now is your confidence in the existence of the Higher reality and your aspiration to this reality.

You should start with yourself, with your personal relationship with God, who is within you. Only then, when you establish your personal relationship with inner God, will your life begin to change. It is the choice that you must make immediately.

You should affirm again and again the Divine principles on the planet — in every sphere of activity, in everything!

It makes sense to devote your being on Earth only to the eternal everlasting values, to something that will stay with you when you leave your earthly school of life and move to the new cycles of the evolutionary development.

Your Faith in the Higher Worlds, in God, will create all the necessary conditions and prerequisites so that your existence in the physical world can become closer to the Higher worlds. You only need to find that point in your being from which the perspective of the eternal Life opens.

There are only two main qualities that lead you out of the labyrinth of illusion like a thread. The first is Faith. The second one is Love.

For some people, Love is in the first place, and Faith is in the second. Others will say that there is no difference between Faith and Love, because the true Faith is always based on Love. Love to God, Love to neighbor, Love to the whole Life.

You only need to believe and live according to the principles that are commanded by the prophets of all times.

Labor itself is of great value. Genuine work is the highest good for the development of a human soul.

Reconsider your attitude toward work.

What matters in the Divine world is a completely different result of your labor: the skills and the invaluable experience that are indispensable for the development of your individuality.

All money, like any other kind of energy, is given to you by God. It is only Him who you should be grateful to for everything: for the food that you eat, for the clothes that you wear, for the shelter that you have, for the Teaching that you get from us.

When you realize your Oneness with every little part of Life and direct your attention to helping those who need your help, you will ascend to the level of consciousness that is necessary at the given stage of your evolution.

You need to look upward, to raise your gaze above the vanity of your surrounding life, and to aspire to look into the future world that is ready to accept your souls for further development.

Your consciousness resembles an unopened bud of a flower. Turn your head toward the sunshine more bravely, and its caressing rays will lovingly do their job of opening the lotus of your Divine consciousness toward the New Day that is coming.

Bravely leave your attachments! Do not be afraid of the changes! Do not be afraid of falling down and getting hurt.

Everything that impedes you from being concentrated on God, on the Higher worlds, has to gradually leave your life.

You should devote more time to your soul, to having conversations with your soul.

The bright spring sun will rise and the snow and ice of your imperfections will melt. Under the caressing rays of the Sun, a new layer of grass and leaves will be formed. Do not be afraid to give up the old and obsolete! Aspire forward toward the new and perfect Divine manifestation in everything.

If your motive is pure and your aspiration is strong, you will overcome time and space, and you will confidently continue your advancement in the open space of this Universe.

Ascend. Cast away your fear and insecurity.
Aspire!
Move ahead!

Improving oneself. You have probably noticed that all the best human qualities come from within you: Love, Mercy, Compassion, care for your neighbors, and Joy. All of these qualities come from your hearts.

Please, keep your consciousness at the highest possible level 24 hours a day.

Do not think about the external. Think about the qualities of your soul. External things will take place on their own if the gold nuggets sparkle inside you, coloring your aura with the golden color of enlightenment.

God uses any conditions, any social system, and any circumstances so that you can develop, so that your souls can develop. It is quite possible for you to develop knight-like qualities of chivalry during these times.

Without the skills of using the sword of knowledge, without saddling the horse of your ego, you will not become the knight of the Word of all times.

Do not be afraid of failures; do not be afraid that you will make a mistake.

When your being is filled with the Divine energy, you are happy because by filling your being, the Divine energy can raise your vibrations to the most beautiful states of joy, love, inner harmony, and peace that are available to you.

The whole mechanism of happy life is inherent inside of you. Why don't you use it?

Do you really think that God will not be able to take care of you when you completely devote yourself to Him? Do you really think that His caring hands will not protect every step that you take when you begin your unstable walk toward the New World?

There is a Law that is in effect in the illusionary world. This Law operates flawlessly and impeccably. The Law says that the things that happen to you are those that you believe in and what you aspire to.

When you harmonize yourselves and come in harmony with the forces of nature, these forces become obedient to you and you can control them.

You need to become more sensitive. More sensitive toward the whole life that exists together with you on Earth and that you do not pay attention to.

None of the entertainments and pleasures of your world can substitute for your soul the co-creation with nature, the elementals, and God. The human is born for creation, and in this way he is similar to God but not by constantly receiving endless pleasures from life.

You need to decide what is more important for you: this world or the Divine world.

The whole seeming diversity of the choices you make every day is reduced to just this one main choice.

If volcanoes can erupt and rocks can come down because of even one inharmonious thought, then it is possible to predict what words can do in your world.

You should wend your way through life carefully. Watch out for even an ant when taking a step. The abuse of the Word is much more severe for your karma.

The only true motives that you should follow in any of your actions on any planes of being must be Mercy, Compassion, selflessness, and your desire to help Life.

Each of your decisions either moves you along the way to the Higher Worlds or makes you slide down the descending spiral. In fact, the motive that drives you while making a decision determines the direction in which you will move.

Everything is possible with God!

The faith in the invisible allows your consciousness to catch the object of your faith, and it starts being attracted to your world.

Do not lose Faith or Hope, and maintain Love in your hearts.

All of you will gain your Victory!

You should not lose your hearts or fall into despondency!

Always Victory! Always Victory! Always Victory!

Not by going wide, but by moving deep you reach the Truth.

Only through renunciation, only through self-sacrifice, only through selfless giving of all your strength to serve your neighbor, can you move along the Divine Path.

Do not think that everything is over. Everything is just starting! Brilliant discoveries are awaiting you in the nearest future!

There might be clouds, there might be a snowstorm, there might be roaring thunder or a hurricane, but no matter what, you know that there is the Sun, and it is always with you.

It is the same in your lives. Despite difficulties, problems, and even miseries, you should know that the Divine part of you is constantly with you.

Anything less than Divine perfection should be left in the past and forgotten.

It is time to move straight up the evolutionary steps.

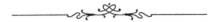

You need to constantly work on your consciousness, every day and day after day.

The only path commanded for your time is the path of perfecting yourself in God.

All your life, you must use every minute of your stay on Earth only for the purpose of concentration on the Supreme. Every day you should devote all your thoughts, feelings, and deeds to God. You should constantly make sure that none of the evil thoughts or desires can seize your consciousness even for a second. You should build a fortress around yourself, an unassailable fortress against anything evil and non-divine that exists in your world, on your planet.

Do not think that you must do some very important job somewhere on the other side of the globe. Most often, you are right where your work is most needed.

You should pay more attention to your inner world and to your inner sensations. If you are attuned with the Divine Truth inside yourselves, then this tuning fork sound of your soul will attract the necessary information to you from the surrounding space.

You should be clearly aware of the connection between all your actions and the consequences to which your actions lead.

Constantly concentrating on the positive and on the desire to help the beings around you and especially your children, can transform the energy of past mistakes and create a new opportunity for the future of your children.

Everything is interconnected in the world, and you should treat everything you do thoughtfully and with due care.

Get involved bravely in forming a new consciousness and a new way of thinking. It is when you, in your consciousness, admit the fact that everything can change — and it can change according to the Divine Law — that these changes will happen.

Aspire to the Divine impressions in your consciousness. Keep the childlike faith in a miracle within yourself, and the miracle will certainly happen!

Do not be afraid of the changes that are coming. Think about the enormous possibilities that are opening up!

Get involved in the work of transforming life on planet Earth based on the Divine principles and Divine guidance!

The choice is hard when there are so many temptations, yet it is the refusal of enticements and overcoming temptations that has always opened the Path of Light.

You have to make a conscious choice and decide what the priority in your life is: you with all your carnal desires or God.

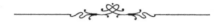

Each of you will face your own choice, but the essence of this choice is always the same: You either choose the illusory world, the world of illusion surrounding you in the physical world, or you choose the real and eternal world.

The power of prayer is the weapon with which you can oppose any violence, any bloodshed, and any injustice that exists in your world.

There cannot be miracles that do not have the support of the Heavens. During your time, there is an opportunity for a miracle to happen. You can foster that miracle with the efforts of your hearts.

The time has come to realize the fact that without the Divine guidance, without following the Divine Law, any further existence of mankind is impossible. Every individual makes his or her own choice what to favor.

You need to make your choice in favor of God and follow this choice day after day. Give up the desires that are tying you to the illusory world.

Bravely expose your being to the winds of change. Fear nothing! Your fears will clear away along with the twilight of your human consciousness when you come out into the sun of your Higher Self.

Take a daring step onto the Path!

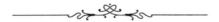

Each one of you is a miracle in the hands of God. Everything is determined only by your consciousness and your aspiration toward the Divine.

All spheres of human activity should be transformed in accordance with the Divine Law; otherwise, they simply cannot exist.

By saving yourselves from the low states of consciousness, you save the whole world because everything is interconnected in our world. A beat of a butterfly's wings is heard as a roar of thunder in the subtle worlds. What then is the effect of your actions, thoughts, and feelings?

Call for help, and the help will come!
Pray for salvation, and the salvation will come!
Trust in God, and God will protect and guide you!
It is only your desire to change that is required.

It is your wish to serve the evolutions of planet Earth that is required.

The time has come for you to make a revolution in your consciousness!

You must find the time to think about the Eternal and the transitory, about the timeless values and momentary fancies, to feel the difference between them and to understand in which direction you wish to move.

The polarity reversal of your consciousness and the centering on eternal values is the stage of the human evolution where mankind is now standing on the threshold.

You need to realize this simple Truth that you are now on the cusp of knowing. Simply accept the existence of the Higher reality in your consciousness.

This will be the necessary and sufficient step that will enable the transformation of everything around you.

Faith in the Higher reality and the aspiration to the Higher worlds are what can take humanity out of sweet dreaming in the illusion.

The time to awaken has come.

The sun of the eternal reality is rising.

Now the time has come to understand that all the changes that are to happen will come to your world from within you. For that, you should come closer to the Divine reality in your consciousness.

Retreat to the silence of your heart; feel the peace and the bliss of eternity. From that point, you will be able to acquire a proper perspective on everything that surrounds you in the external world.

Any of the most subtle impulses of your soul causes inevitable changes in the physical world. If you experience the states of happiness, love and peace, then you exert influence on vast distances around you and, perhaps, even on the whole planet.

All of you will have to make your final choices in the near future about which path to follow: whether to go along the Divine Path or to continue manifesting your will on defending the path that leads nowhere.

There is nothing in your lives more important than following and obeying the Will of God.

This simple Truth can work miracles on all planes of Being when it takes hold of a human individual.

Therefore, your Faith — Faith and Love — is what should always be with you. That is what should guide all your actions and deeds in the physical plane.

Everything can be overcome, and everything is possible with God!

What man is unable to do — God can do — even that which seems impossible from the point of view of human logic.

Just let God into your consciousness — the rest He will do Himself.

When there is a sense of reality, Divinity within you, everything that is less than Divine perfection will go past your consciousness, leaving no traces in it. Then you will aspire to your Victory, to your Freedom from the chains of matter.

Those who will be able to keep their consciousness on the vibrations of Joy, Love, harmony, and happiness, will be able to fully enjoy the upcoming changes. Those who are in the old habit of being attuned to hostility, doubts, and fear, will soon be able to easily give up these energies of the preceding age.

Joy and Love come to you when your Faith is steadfast, when you rely on God and the Ascended Hosts in your consciousness.

Guard yourselves against any negative energies of the past.

Courageously enter the New Age, the Age of Aquarius!

Welcome the new energies, the energies of regeneration, and follow them!

You need to accept the new. You need to control every movement of your thoughts and cut off from yourselves everything that does not lead you along the path of your ascension to the Truth.

The time is coming when the concentration on one's narrow private interests comes into conflict with the call of the time. The time is coming when only the collective consciousness, the consciousness focused on caring about others, the Common Good of the planet, and every living being on Earth, will have prospects for its development.

There is no place in the future world for a consciousness that is concentrated only on itself and the whims of its ego. The Path to evolution opens up only to those whose consciousness is able to expand the range of its attention to the Divine horizons. This is precisely the situation that the world is in now.

Everything is very simple. And the choice is very simple: You either choose God or you choose your mortal consciousness, your ego.

What you give preference to is what you will eventually be left with.

If you manage to rise to the Divine level in your human consciousness, then you will acquire immortality and eternal Life as your reward.

You yourself determine your future Path by your own choice.

A Divine miracle is beside you. It is ready to be manifested but the energy of your prayers and your positive aspirations for happiness, Bliss, and Good are needed to manifest the miracle.

Let God into your life.

When your consciousness is able to rise to the Divine level, all the necessary transformations in all spheres of society will occur as if by themselves.

There is a mechanism hidden within you which will enable you to find the way out of the most difficult situation. A particle of God is dazzling within you. You should regularly devote some time during the day to your communication with God. You should continuously cultivate the feeling of the Divine within yourselves.

When God is able to be constantly present near you wherever you are — outside, at work, at home, in the store — everything around you will start changing, and your life will change its course and direct itself along the Divine Path of development.

Change your consciousness, make it closer to God, and everything in your lives will change within the lifetime of one generation.

You need to illuminate the space around you with the Divine Light emanating from the innermost depths of your being, and then you will obtain the understanding and knowledge that are necessary for you to come out of the darkness into the Light.

Your aspiration to the Common Good will be supported by all the Heavens and the energies of the coming New Age.

You need to regain harmony with the Divine part of yourselves. Only from this point of harmony with the Divine world will you be able to see the events of your world from the correct point of view.

Transformation of consciousness and thinking — that is what must be done first of all at this time!

Do not be afraid of anything! Those who are with God have nothing to fear!

It is exactly now when the time has come for you to take action. Your inner attainments, which are manifested as the flames of your heart, as the radiance of your aura, and as a halo around your head, should be used by you now.

It is exactly now that you must work hard. The future of planet Earth depends on the effectiveness of the work that you are doing now to overcome any negative states of being.

As light-bearers, your primary task is to project proper models into the world. For this, you need to rely on the inner knowledge that comes from within your hearts.

Do not forget about God in the bustle of the day. If, in the prime of the day when dull energies cover you up completely, you are able to keep the memory of God at least in the corner of your consciousness, then no storms and stresses of life can threaten you.

Always preserve the purity of your heart, no matter what life situations you are facing. This will help you to keep the right direction in your life and always follow the higher Path destined for you by God!

At every moment of time, you are creating. You are controlling your energy. You only need to attune to God in order for your energy channels to be always within the Divine channel.

Everyone who is able to maintain the balance of energies within them and to keep the state of inner peace and harmony at this time will be the guarantor for the sustainable development of the entire humankind.

The level of consciousness is what determines the outer conditions, controls the manifestation of the outer forces, and forms the circumstances in the physical world.

You always have the opportunity to stop and ponder whether you are acting in accordance with God or against God.

Therefore, invite God and the Ascended Hosts in to your life more often, ask for their Divine instruction and Divine guidance, and you will always receive them.

You must strive to acquire a point of balance, a foothold within yourselves. This is vital because if you do it, if you find the point of balance within yourselves, then you will always be calm even when the whole world is in a storm.

This point of balance is the connection with your authentic essence, with your Divine essence, with God within you.

When you acquire this state of balance and peace, you will win a great victory!

Everything has meaning in your life.

Everything should be treated very attentively.

Sometimes, one object that you fix your eyes on at a difficult moment is enough for your vibrations to change and for you to enter the field of high, Divine vibrations.

Now the time has come when much depends on each choice of yours, on each step of yours, on each thought of yours.
The circumstances on the planet have changed.
It is necessary to be very cautious.

Your consciousness is something that either brings you nearer to God or moves you away from God. Thus, everything in your life is determined by the level of your consciousness.

Courage is the quality that is indispensable for you!

Joy must be with you always!
Your being must be open to the changes.
The New Age will be characterized by tolerance, freedom, and independence.

You will have independence from the external circumstances. You will be able to manifest your Divine nature more freely and courageously.

When you inseparably connect your life with God and the Masters, when the Divine Law governs your life, what can obstruct your path?

Any barriers, any difficulties, you will easily overcome.

All the obstacles can be overcome when you walk along with God.

The inner Light will illuminate the Path for you in the most difficult life situations.

The whole Path lies within you. Your energy system, when liberated from the patterns of mass consciousness, will be able to attune you. A gigantic potential of self-attunement to the Higher worlds is concealed within you.

The Path lying ahead of you does not unfold outside of yourselves. This Path reveals itself within you. This Path is the changing of your consciousness.

You direct the process of changing your consciousness yourselves.

Like a sailboat, your being must put the wind of the Universal Law in its sails.

You must decide who will be the chief in your life: you or God.

You must make the decision within your being and submit your whole life to God and to the fulfillment of His needs and requirements.

Everything in this world reveals itself from within. Such is the Law. The illusion obediently turns the side to you that you expect to receive from it.

Change yourself, aspire, and you will be blessed with the golden robe of Buddha and the treasure of the Divine Wisdom.

Do not hesitate to act for the benefit of the evolutions of planet Earth!

All the changes will come into the physical world from the innermost of your being. You are the people whose mission it is to spread the Divine world from within you into the outer world.

You will be able to save yourself and your soul only if you wholeheartedly aspire to God and to the observance of the Divine Law.

Remember that you attract from the space exactly what you send there. It depends solely on you what energies you send to the world and in what state you reside.

You become the person who you think you are. This is the Law of space in which you live.

Most importantly, you should convince yourself to believe in the fact that God is with you. What can happen to you in your life if God Himself is staying with you and cares for you?

Residing in God and having a feeling of the Divine are simply a state of your consciousness. If you wish to constantly reside in God, you will let Him first into your heart, and then, after some time, He will occupy your whole being. Like the Sun that is illuminating the whole Earth and everything around, God will shine through you upon the entire world.

Residing in God means that you constantly have a good and stable mood, with joy and love overwhelming you.

God is always beside you. Do not be stubborn like little children. Allow God into your lives!

Now!

It is necessary to transition from the external to the inner knowledge. The external is only an impulse for your consciousness to plunge into the space of communication with God who resides within your own being.

Your task is to simply return the true values into your life. The call of duty, dignity, devotion, faith, and love are among these values.

Therefore, please memorize your Code of Honor which in its first lines reads that there is nothing in your illusory world that would have a greater priority and be of higher value than God and obedience to the Divine Law.

On the basis of this statement, all the rest will become clear to you, and it will acquire a different meaning.

Your life itself is of a lower value than God and obedience to the Divine Law because by sacrificing your life for the sake of God, you acquire eternal Life.

The main choice that you are making in your life and from one life to another is the choice either in favor of the Divine world or in favor of the illusory world.

Everything depends only on your aspiration and the motive by which you are guided in your life.

The outer obediently repeats your inner state. Therefore, your whole concern must be in your following the Law of God in your hearts, in your inner space.

By changing yourself, you will change the world around you.

The sun of your Divinity must illuminate your mind and all your thoughts and feelings. And this will happen.

You can show the Path to many lost souls. Pray for the enlightenment of humanity and forgive everyone.

You should constantly think about God in order to return Him into your lives!

This decision is very simple: If you wish to be happy, be happy!

Every day, you must devote some time for spiritual practices. You cannot miss a single day, because if you stop pedaling while going up the mountain, you will slide down to the foot of the mountain, and you will have to start your ascension over again.

There are eternal values that stay with you throughout your entire journey on the evolutionary path. These qualities are known to everyone and do not need to be justified: Kindness, Mercy, Compassion, Love, nobility, courage, devotion, aspiration, and constancy.

You have to return to God. This means that you are to carry out a revolution in your consciousness in the near future.

The Divine guidance is not manifested from the outside but from the inside of human individuals.

That is why the focus of attention must be redirected from the external to the internal.

If you do not think about the eternal, then you will not be able to live eternal lives.

If you do not devote time in solitude for thinking over your qualities, then you will not be able to develop your Divinity.

All the keys and mechanisms are hidden within you, and only you make this decision. Some people go along a wide road to nowhere, while others find a narrow path leading to eternity.

The choice is yours.

Virtually, you create your own happiness.

You just need to constantly maintain awareness and constantly feel your Oneness with God.

Only your devotion to the Will of God!
Only your determination to gain the victory!
Only your desire to withstand!

Every minute and every second of your embodiment, you must be aware of your connection with God. Only in this case will you get the invulnerable protection of Light!

Only in this case will you be able to advance toward your victory!

One can withstand the onslaught of a thousand if he is with God!

Nothing matters in the situation that has formed on Earth except for one thing: You must return God into your lives!

At any cost, even at the cost of your own life.

No hour of your life should be lived without God.

Your physical body will be left in the soil; your task is to save your soul.

That is why all wise men of all times preferred to lose their bodies but to save their souls.

Only with the power of your Spirit will you be able to stop the external opposition and the internal confrontation of the negative energies that are still inherent to you.

You must take action; you must be actively involved in the external activities and gain your experience.

Only collective, positive actions are capable of overcoming the existing negative tendency in the world.

You must return the Divine order into your world!
You are responsible for planet Earth!
The time for your actions has come! Now!

There is so much that is beautiful and charming in this world. There is so much of what God has given to mankind absolutely free as a Divine gift. These gifts are the sunrises and sunsets, the warmth of the sun, the song of the birds, the blooming of the flowers, the sound of the wind, and the babbling of the streams.

God has given so much to mankind!

That is why your main objective will be to bring back into your world the Divine Truth, and after that, the Divine harmony and Divine peace will come back into your world, and your being will become filled with meaning.

There are two main approaches in all areas of human life: the Divine and the non-divine.

All the decisions that you make during the day are divided into the Divine and non-divine ones.

Do not get involved in the negative states of consciousness, constantly maintain your positive consciousness, get rid of all non-divine manifestations in your life, and surround yourselves with the Divine models of Light.

You become what you absorb.

The mechanism of controlling all the processes taking place on Earth is within your being. There is a kind of switch or a valve in each of you that either forces you to make Divine decisions or to follow a non-divine path.

The first and the most important step will be to believe in the existence of the Divine world and to wish to serve the Light.

When you make a Divine choice and act according to the highest moral models, you raise your vibrations and ascend along the spiral of evolutionary development.

You must maintain your independence and absolute devotion to the Supreme ideals in any of your surroundings.

You are warriors in your world!

You are the warriors of Light!

You are the knights of Spirit!

No matter what the circumstances of your life are, never forget about that!

Your duty is to Serve God and all of Life!

When the rays of the dawn of the Divine consciousness start illuminating the twilight of your being with the Light of reason, you acquire the distinction between the Light and the dark, the reality and the illusion.

Every day you make your choice, the only choice between the world of God and the world of illusion. There are millions of choices, but the essence of them is reduced to the only choice: whether you choose the Eternity or you choose decay.

Every day of your life must be devoted only to God, to God residing within you, and to God residing in every living being.

Only one thought must be in your mind when you wake up: "I am with God!"

Only this thought can shield you from the forces of illusion throughout your day.

Only permanent concentration on God can get you out of the nets of illusion.

Tirelessly, every day ask God to be with you and to guide your whole life and all your choices.

Only God can help you and your soul at this difficult time in the twilight of human consciousness.

The state of inner bliss, peace, harmony, and Love is sometimes more valuable and more rare than material wealth at this time on Earth.

A human needs so little to be happy. You just need to be attuned to the Divine and to live for the sake of your neighbor.

All depends on your sustaining the inner balance.

Your task is to transform any negativity into Love and Mercy by the flames of your hearts.

Each of you is part of the energy system of planet Earth. The frequency at which you vibrate during most of the day affects the general energy field of the planet.

When you can retain Love and Joy in your hearts despite the negative influences from the outside, you submerge yourself into the positive energies of rejuvenation and create a positive mindset that works for the entire planet.

Your self-improvement, the eradication of your imperfections, requires a lot of effort.

The only person in this world whom you can change is yourself.

Change yourselves, and the entire world will change!

Human spiritual achievements are determined by only one thing: the ability to maintain the state of inner peace and Oneness with the Creator despite any external circumstances.

Every person has a chance to change the vector of his or her aspirations toward the Divine at any moment.

You simply need to constantly think about God and devote all the activities of your day to God.

Try to do all the things in your life only in accordance with the Divine vision.

Open your hearts to Love, and send a small part of your Love to each suffering heart in your world.

This will not be hard for you, will it?

We can change any situation on planet Earth with our mutual efforts.

You must be firm in your faith, and with your faith you will be able to let so much Love into your world that the hearts of many people will change.

Everything can be changed, beloved.

Everything is possible with God's help, absolutely everything. You just need to focus all your efforts on God entering your lives and guiding you in all your deeds and actions.

Every day and from day to day.

Think about the Divine Love that is growing in your heart every day.

Always reside in Love, and everything around you will start changing.

There is always an opportunity to take an easier path. However, that opportunity is open only to those few who are sincerely following the Ancient Teaching and have forever tied their lives with God.

First, the choice is made in the plane of thoughts and feelings, and then that choice comes down to the physical plane.

Within just a few years, faith in God alone is able to return both the Divine models and the Moral Law into your life.

It is never too late.
You may turn around and get back to the Divine Path of development at any point of your life journey.

There is no such negative quality or fault that cannot be overcome with the help of God.

God always gives you an opportunity to cope with any of your faults independently.

Then, when you are able to manifest only Divine qualities, the whole world will turn its Divine side toward you.

Every one of you needs to deal only with yourself, only with your own inner state, and the world around you will change by itself.

The world is on the threshold of the New Age. It will come inevitably, like the sun rises at the end of the night, no matter how dark it was.

Always remember that the outer is determined by the inner.

Your complete readiness is needed!

Your complete concentration on the Supreme.

The inner determines the outer.

Right now is the time for your work for the good of the evolution of planet Earth!

Only inner balance, even if the whole world collapses.

As soon as you make your choice in favor of God, all the Ascended Hosts stand up to protect your soul, no matter what the external circumstances are.

Therefore, remember God every moment of your life and devote your entire life to God and to the fulfillment of His Law!

We provide our help and support for you in the form of these Messages. You should treat everything that is given to you with due care.

Collect every pearl and every precious jewel contained in each Message, and store them in a secret place. When an even darker and gloomier time comes, take out these treasures; they will be able to save your Life — not the life that exists in the physical plane but the Life that is eternal. Your consciousness is just a pass into the eternal world. A person who can bloom as a beautiful lotus of the Divine consciousness in the swamp of life deserves to enter the eternal Life.

The perishable cannot enter my world. Only the imperishable, immortal part of you can exist in my world.

For that, you should take care of your immortal part now. Do not collect the treasures that belong to your world; collect only the treasures of the Divine Wisdom which are of great value in all the worlds.

From the book
Words of Wisdom

About Tatyana N. Mickushina's Books

Tatyana N. Mickushina is the founder of the philosophical-ethical Teaching aimed at restoring morality in society. The Teaching has been given through her by the Masters of mankind in the form of talks or Messages.

The three main pillars upon which the Teaching is based are the Supreme Moral Law, the Law of Karma, and the Law of Reincarnation.

In a simple form, through their Messages, the Masters of Wisdom allow us to understand why we should be moral and adhere to the Supreme Moral Law in our lives; why it is always advantageous to be moral. This knowledge is naturally derived from the knowledge of the Law of Karma (the Law of cause and effect) and the Law of Reincarnation (the Law of the Evolution of the soul). When we come to understand that we live not one but many lives, that all our thoughts, feelings, and deeds at the present point in time determine our near and remote future, we begin to treat the surrounding life and our reactions to life events more consciously and responsibly.

The treasure of the Masters of Wisdom given in the form of Messages is presented in the books *Words of Wisdom*. The *Words of Wisdom* series consists of cycles of Messages in the same chronological order as they were given to Tatyana N. Mickushina. A thoughtful reader will find pearls of Wisdom in them.

Below are several important concepts of this Teaching:

• Everything that exists in the world is God, and the whole universe is developing based solely on the Divine Laws. The meaning of a person's life is to obtain his or her Divine nature and to return to the Father's House. If one does not aspire to develop their Divine nature, then by doing so he or she violates the Law of the Creator.

• Among the multitude of the Divine Laws, there are three main Laws: the Law of Reincarnation, the Law of Karma, and the Supreme Moral Law. If humankind does not learn these Laws, then they will not be able to change themselves and the world for the better, and they will degrade.

- We can change the world preeminently by changing our consciousness because the surrounding world is only a mirror that reflects our consciousness. The more perfect our consciousness, the more perfect the world around us becomes. It is not possible for mankind to continue its evolution in any other way.

These truths unfold in the Messages through many aspects of the Teaching: in the Teaching about the changing of consciousness, in the Teaching on Love, in the Teaching on Freedom, in the Teaching on non-violence, in the Teaching on happiness, in the Teaching on the Path of Initiations, and in many others.

From the Editor.

Ascended Masters' Messages

TREASURES
OF DIVINE WISDOM

Tatyana N. Mickushina

Translator: Hanna Mityashina

Buy Books by T. N. Mickushina on Amazon:
amazon.com/author/tatyana_mickushina

Websites:
http://sirius-eng.net/ (English version)
http://sirius-ru.net/ or http://sirius-net.org
(Russian version)

Illustrations: belchonok © 123RF.com
Konstantin Kulikov © 123RF.com